FREDDY AND THE BAND

Published in the United States of America
ISBN Paperback: 979-8-89091-281-7
ISBN Hardback: 979-8-89091-282-4
ISBN eBook: 979-8-89091-283-1

ReadersMagnet, LLC
10620 Treena Street, Suite 230 | San Diego, California, 92131 USA
1.619.354.2643 | www.readersmagnet.com

FREDDY AND THE BAND

AUTHOR & CREATOR:
BRYN ELIZABETH COOPER
ILLUSTRATOR: MICHAEL JAKE TE

ReadersMagnet, LLC

To the parent or guardian:
Please note, all colored words are misspelled intentionally.

This book is good for Ages 2 and up.

JUST SKATIN' ALONG, SINGIN' A SONG
DREAMIN' OF BEING IN A BAND
FREDDY MAKES UP HIS MIND TO FOLLOW HIS HEART
AND BE A ROCKSTAR AS HE'D ALWAYS PLANNED

SO FREDDY GOES HOME AND CHANGES HIS CLOTHES

AND GETS READY TO HIT THE STREETS

LET'S FOLLOW FREDDY ON HIS ADVENTURE

AND SEE WHO FREDDY MEETS

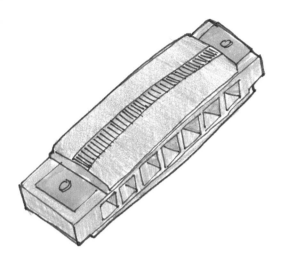

HIPSTER HIPPO IS IN THE HOUSE

HITTIN' THE HARMONICA WITH A GROOVE

HE'S BIG LIKE EVERY HIPPO IS

BUT HE CAN DANCE AND HE CAN MOVE

THERE'S SUBWAY STEPHANIE, THE SINGIN' SKUNK

WHO LIVES UNDERNEATH THE STREET

SHE LOST HER SMELL AND IS DOIN' SO WELL

GOIN' COUNTRY AND SMELLIN' SO SWEET

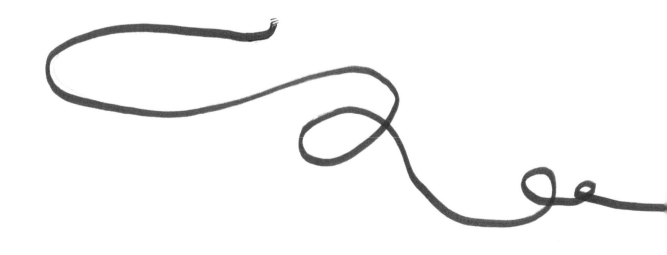

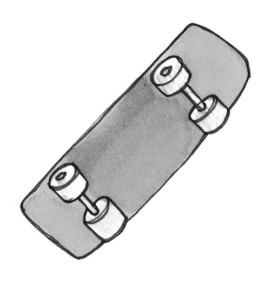

KANGAROO KEVIN AND HIS KRAZY WAYS

KICKS THE KEYBOARD INTO THE AIR

THIS 80'S DUDE IS KRUSHIN' IT

SPREADIN' MUSIC EVERYWHERE

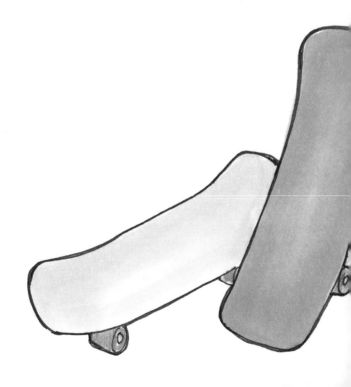

GARY THE GRINDIN' GATOR

PLAYS A TINY LITTLE GUITAR

WITH HIS REAL SHORT ARMS, HE CAN JAM ALL NIGHT

AND HE LOOKS A LITTLE BIZARRE

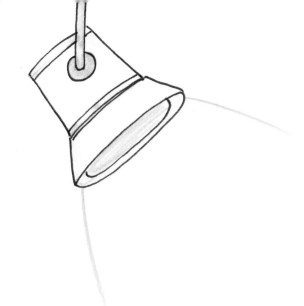

DISCO DANNY, THE DRUMMIN' DONKEY

LOVES LISTENING TO HIS BEATS

BUDS AND A DURAG ON HIS HEAD

ELECTRICITY IN HIS FEET!

TAMBOURINE TAMMY TEARS UP THE TOWN

GETTIN' NOTICED AT EVERY TURN

THIS TIGER IS SHAKIN' OUT TAMBORINE TUNES

MAKIN' SONGS ALL THE KIDS CAN LEARN

FREDDY KNOWS HE WILL NEED STUFF FOR THE BAND

CALLING "RAMAZON", HE PLACES HIS ORDER

HE HAS ONE MORE SINGER LEFT TO FIND

AND SEES ONE PLAYIN' ON THE CORNER

IT'S ROXANNE THE ROCK AND ROLL RABBIT

WITH HER FAMOUS FOOT-TAPPIN' HABIT

SHE SINGS SO CUTE IN HER POLKA-DOT SUIT

FREDDY THINKS SHE OUGHTA' HAVE IT!

SO THE ANIMALS DECIDE TO GIVE IT A TRY

AND HEAD TOWARDS FREDDY'S GARAGE

THE "RAMAZON" GUY WAS DROPPIN' OFF BOXES

BECAUSE FREDDY HAD TAKEN CHARGE

YOU SEE, FREDDY TOOK A CHANCE AND PUT TOGETHER

ALL THE MUSICAL TALENT HE COULD MEET

WROTE SOME TUNES AND STARTED A BAND

WITH A HOOK THAT IS DOWN WITH THE BEAT . . . .

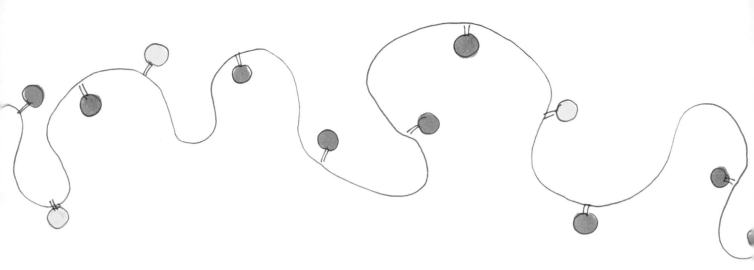

NOW, WITH ALL THEIR DIFFERENT SHAPES AND SIZES

THE ANIMALS WERE ABLE TO MOVE

FREDDY TURNED HIS GARAGE INTO A CLUB

WHERE ALL THE ANIMALS COULD GROOVE

... AND THE BAND SINGS ...

"WHATEVER YOU DREAM
YOU CAN MAKE IT COME TRUE
DO YOU AND DO IT OUTLOUD
WITH A LIL' HARD WORK AND SOME BOOM IN YOUR BOUNCE
YOU'LL WALK AWAY FEELIN' SO PROUD

AND ALWAYS REMEMBER TO BE KIND TO ANIMALS
YOU'D BE SURPRISED WHO YOU MIGHT MEET
YOU MAY FIND YOUR DREAMS ARE ALL COMIN' TRUE
SINGIN' SONGS WITH THE BAND ON THE STREET"

YES, FREDDY MADE HIS DREAM COME TRUE
JUMPED IN AND TOOK COMMAND
MUSIC HAS ALWAYS BEEN HIS THING
AND NOW HE'S ROCKIN' WITH HIS BAND!

Milton Keynes UK
Ingram Content Group UK Ltd.
UKRC032327291123
433523UK00006B/82